# Unwavering Faith

## jesus every day

*Devotional Guide*

CANDACE | DaySpring

candacecbure.com | dayspring.com

# WELCOME!

I can't tell you how much reading the Bible has changed my life. In my marriage, in my career, in my role as a parent, and in everything I do, the real glue that keeps it all together is Jesus, so when I have questions, I go to the Bible.

You see, I used to compartmentalize my life. My faith in God would be in one box, my work in another, my family in another. But as I read more of the Bible and as my relationship with Jesus deepened, I realized that He wants to be involved in *every* detail of my life.

You don't have to wait for something big to happen to talk to God or to include Him in the details of your life. He's already with you—loving, strengthening, encouraging, and guiding you every second of every day. Whether you're having the best day ever or you're facing the worst times of your life, God is there for you. He wants to help you develop an unwavering faith that withstands the trials, temptations, doubts, and fears of life.

As you journey through this guide, remember to pray. It doesn't matter where you are on your walk with God. You can ask Him to speak to you through the words of the Bible—His true and constant words. So let's go! Let's see what God has to teach us through this adventure.

In this together, Candace

# Before You Get Started on This Adventure

$\mathcal{H}$ere's the deal. You're picking this book up and are either super excited to dig in or wondering if you really want to start this journey with me. I get it. Trust me, I do. And while I can tell you that this study can undoubtedly change your life, you may not be eager to jump in based on my enthusiasm alone. But would you do me a favor? Would you at least read through this first section before you put this book back on the shelf?

Before jumping into it, you might be wondering why the Bible is worth reading or what all the talk about being "saved" means. You may feel like you'll never measure up to God's standards—that there's no hope for you—so why even try? Or maybe you feel like you're doing just fine and life is actually pretty good, so why would you need to dig deep into God's Word?

Wherever you are in your spiritual journey, I want you to know you're not alone. In this first section, I've answered some questions people typically ask me about my Christian faith. I hope these answers will be helpful to you too.

# Why should I read and study the Bible?

The world is full of all kinds of books that tell stories, teach concepts, inspire, and entertain. Heck, I've even written a few of them! Many books have influenced the world throughout history, but none compare with the Bible.

We all love a good story, right? While the Bible is full of history, wisdom, guidelines, and poetry, it's actually the epic story about all of creation and time from the beginning to the end. In the Bible, God is the ultimate storyteller—He shares His plan, His story, and His design for the world and for humanity.

The story begins with God creating His beloved humanity—Adam and Eve—in His image. But they destroyed their relationship with Him by choosing power instead of trusting in Him. Then the rest of the Bible—the greatest love story ever told— continues as God sets His plan in motion to bring His people back to Himself.

While there are other books that claim to be "holy," and even some that may contain useful ideas or wise words, no other book explains so clearly humanity's desperate need for rescue and how God Himself came to the rescue by sending His only Son, Jesus. No other book is so transformational because no other book shows us how much we are *loved* by our Creator.

# What does it mean to be "saved"?

When followers of Jesus talk about being saved, we mean that Jesus rescued us from the ultimate consequence of sin—eternal separation from God—and our lives are no longer controlled by sin or filled with darkness, hopelessness, shame, guilt, and fear.

Jesus shines His light, freedom, joy, peace, and hope into our lives. God doesn't want sin to have any control over us. He wants to have a relationship with us. He wants us to live full, abundant, joyful lives that reflect His goodness back to others! That's why Jesus came—to save us from the punishment we deserve because of our sin and to give us new life.

Being saved doesn't mean we are spared from all suffering in our lives. But it does mean we have God's presence with us and the promise of spending forever with Him—an eternity free from all pain and suffering. Jesus is ready to save us the moment we open our hearts to Him and accept His unconditional love for us.

## What if I don't need to be "saved"?

I get this too—you're a good person, you help others, you live honestly, you probably donate time and money to charity, and you're not hurting anyone. Why do you need to be "saved"? Compared to others, you're practically a saint! But God's standards are different from human standards. If we just compare ourselves to other people, it's easy to think we're good enough. But when we compare ourselves to God's standards, we fall miserably short. Every. Single. Time.

We all deserve God's judgment. Because He is holy, He cannot allow sin anywhere near Him. Because of sin, we cannot earn our way to having a relationship with God. Our sin separates us from our Creator. God says that if we break even one commandment, it's as if we're guilty of breaking them all. There isn't one of us who can say we are sinless. And doing good things to earn God's approval doesn't erase our sinfulness either. But because God loves us, He sent His Son, Jesus, to die so that all people—the bad, the good, and everyone in between—could have a relationship with Him.

*B*ecause I believe the Bible shows us who Jesus is and how we can have a relationship with Him, I want to help you get to know Him too. That's what this study guide is all about.

## How do I use this study guide?

Here's how it works: each day has a reading from the Bible and then some questions to help you think about and apply the biblical concepts. It's that simple! There's no "right" answer, and you can add your own questions and thoughts at any point, on any page.

Ideally, this is a personal journey where God will speak directly to your heart. But going through the study with friends can bring you encouragement and help you connect with others in really valuable ways. If you'd like, you could complete a day's study alone and then come together with a group of friends to discuss what God is showing you. You decide!

## Let's do this!

As you go through each day's study, pray through it. Don't just complete it so you can check it off your to-do list. And don't look to me to tell you the answers or what to think; look to the Word and ask God to speak to you. Lastly, don't be afraid. The most repeated command in the Bible is "Do not fear," and one of the most common promises from God is "I am with you." So jump into this adventure and ask God what He wants to reveal to you.

Whether you are new to the Bible or super familiar with it, I can tell you this: God's Word is living and active. It will bring you life, and you will thrive every day as you find truth, peace, and hope within its pages. Let's go!

# Our Need for a Savior

# ROMANS 7:15—25 (NIV)

I do not understand what I do. For what I want to do I do not do, but what I hate I do. And if I do what I do not want to do, I agree that the law is good. As it is, it is no longer I myself who do it, but it is sin living in me. For I know that good itself does not dwell in me, that is, in my sinful nature. For I have the desire to do what is good, but I cannot carry it out. For I do not do the good I want to do, but the evil I do not want to do—this I keep on doing. Now if I do what I do not want to do, it is no longer I who do it, but it is sin living in me that does it.

So I find this law at work: Although I want to do good, evil is right there with me. For in my inner being I delight in God's law; but I see another law at work in me, waging war against the law of my mind and making me a prisoner of the law of sin at work within me. What a wretched man I am! Who will rescue me from this body that is subject to death? Thanks be to God, who delivers me through Jesus Christ our Lord!

So then, I myself in my mind am a slave to God's law, but in my sinful nature a slave to the law of sin.

*How do you respond when you need help? Do you readily acknowledge your need for help,*

*or do you try to fix things on your own? Why?*

*In these verses, Paul, the author of Romans, describes his struggle with his sinful nature.*

*How would you describe your struggle with sin, or the wrong things you don't want to do?*

*How does it make you feel knowing that Jesus is the One who can rescue you from sin?*

YOU DON'T REALIZE JESUS IS ALL YOU *need* UNTIL JESUS IS ALL YOU *have.*

— TIM KELLER

*In which areas of your life are you struggling with sin—either doing what you know is wrong or not doing what you know is right? How can you depend on Jesus to help you today?*

---

---

---

---

---

---

---

---

---

---

---

---

---

---

---

*A note from Candace*

Not every day will be a "fully expectant and trusting God" kinda day; still, let's try. Let's ask Him to help us and look to Him with a measure of hope and faith for the next twenty-four hours. Who knows? Maybe this will be the day that we knock out that sin, temptation, or habit with God's strength.

# Foundation of Faith

# LUKE 6:43—49 (NLT)

"A good tree can't produce bad fruit, and a bad tree can't produce good fruit. A tree is identified by its fruit. Figs are never gathered from thornbushes, and grapes are not picked from bramble bushes. A good person produces good things from the treasury of a good heart, and an evil person produces evil things from the treasury of an evil heart. What you say flows from what is in your heart.

"So why do you keep calling Me 'Lord, Lord!' when you don't do what I say? I will show you what it's like when someone comes to Me, listens to My teaching, and then follows it. It is like a person building a house who digs deep and lays the foundation on solid rock. When the floodwaters rise and break against that house, it stands firm because it is well built. But anyone who hears and doesn't obey is like a person who builds a house right on the ground, without a foundation. When the floods sweep down against that house, it will collapse into a heap of ruins."

*What ideas, concepts, or beliefs do people build their lives on?*

*Do you relate more to the person who built a house on the rock*

*or the person who built a house with no foundation? Why?*

*How do you think following Jesus' teachings helps you build a solid foundation of faith?*

WHEN

*faith*

IS YOUR

FOUNDATION,

*you're*

UNSHAKABLE.

*What practical steps can you take to build your life on a solid foundation of faith?*

_Your biggest takeaway_

# God's Gift of Grace

# EPHESIANS 2:1—10 (CSB)

You were dead in your trespasses and sins in which you previously lived according to the ways of this world, according to the ruler of the power of the air, the spirit now working in the disobedient. We too all previously lived among them in our fleshly desires, carrying out the inclinations of our flesh and thoughts, and we were by nature children under wrath as the others were also. But God, who is rich in mercy, because of His great love that He had for us, made us alive with Christ even though we were dead in trespasses. You are saved by grace! He also raised us up with Him and seated us with Him in the heavens in Christ Jesus, so that in the coming ages He might display the immeasurable riches of His grace through His kindness to us in Christ Jesus. For you are saved by grace through faith, and this is not from yourselves; it is God's gift—not from works, so that no one can boast. For we are His workmanship, created in Christ Jesus for good works, which God prepared ahead of time for us to do.

*When did someone bless you or do something good for you even though you didn't deserve it?*

*Nothing we do on our own can make us right with God. How does it make*

*you feel knowing that God's grace has made you right with Him?*

*God's grace is a gift from Him. It's when we enjoy God's approval—not because of anything we've done*

*but because of His goodness and love. What does this mean to you?*

WE ARE NOT SAVED
BY OUR GIVING,
WE ARE SAVED BY
*God's*
*giving.*

— A. W. PINK

*How can you give the gift of grace to others, doing for others what they cannot do for themselves?*

_____
_____
_____
_____
_____
_____
_____
_____
_____
_____
_____
_____
_____
_____
_____

*Your biggest takeaway*

# Losing Our Life

Once when Jesus was praying in private and His disciples were with Him, He asked them, "Who do the crowds say I am?"

They replied, "Some say John the Baptist; others say Elijah; and still others, that one of the prophets of long ago has come back to life."

"But what about you?" He asked. "Who do you say I am?"

Peter answered, "God's Messiah."

Jesus strictly warned them not to tell this to anyone. And He said, "The Son of Man must suffer many things and be rejected by the elders, the chief priests and the teachers of the law, and He must be killed and on the third day be raised to life."

Then He said to them all: "Whoever wants to be My disciple must deny themselves and take up their cross daily and follow Me. For whoever wants to save their life will lose it, but whoever loses their life for Me will save it. What good is it for someone to gain the whole world, and yet lose or forfeit their very self? Whoever is ashamed of Me and My words, the Son of Man will be ashamed of them when He comes in His glory and in the glory of the Father and of the holy angels."

*How do you feel when you lose something?*

*How do you feel when you find it?*

*Losing our life to find it seems contradictory. What do you think Jesus meant by this?*

*How do you think giving up your life to follow Jesus can actually end up saving your life?*

TAKE UP YOUR

*cross*

AND FOLLOW

*Jesus.*

*What are some things in your life that God may be asking you to lay down, lose, or let go of in order to know Him more? If you'd like, take a moment to ask for His help and strength to let go.*

_A note from Candace_

Here's an amazing truth: sometimes we have to let go of something we have for something better. But that is *hard*, right? Make no mistake about it—letting go of our lives to follow Jesus takes courage and self-discipline, but the rewards are eternal!

# Made in God's Image

# GENESIS 1:26—31 (NLT)

Then God said, "Let Us make human beings in Our image, to be like Us. They will reign over the fish in the sea, the birds in the sky, the livestock, all the wild animals on the earth, and the small animals that scurry along the ground."

> So God created human beings in His own image.
> In the image of God He created them;
> male and female He created them.

Then God blessed them and said, "Be fruitful and multiply. Fill the earth and govern it. Reign over the fish in the sea, the birds in the sky, and all the animals that scurry along the ground."

Then God said, "Look! I have given you every seed-bearing plant throughout the earth and all the fruit trees for your food. And I have given every green plant as food for all the wild animals, the birds in the sky, and the small animals that scurry along the ground—everything that has life." And that is what happened.

Then God looked over all He had made, and He saw that it was very good!

And evening passed and morning came, marking the sixth day.

*What does it mean to you to be created in God's image?*

*According to these verses, what are some of the responsibilities God gave to humans?*

*God viewed His creation as "good."*

*How does your view of creation compare with God's view?*

WE REFLECT
THE CHARACTER
OF OUR

*Creator.*

*How does the realization that you are created in God's image affect the way you view yourself? How does it affect the way you view other people?*

_____
_____
_____
_____
_____
_____
_____
_____
_____
_____
_____
_____
_____
_____
_____
_____

*Your biggest takeaway*

# Learning to Love

# I JOHN 4:7–16 (NIV)

Dear friends, let us love one another, for love comes from God. Everyone who loves has been born of God and knows God. Whoever does not love does not know God, because God is love. This is how God showed His love among us: He sent His one and only Son into the world that we might live through Him. This is love: not that we loved God, but that He loved us and sent His Son as an atoning sacrifice for our sins. Dear friends, since God so loved us, we also ought to love one another. No one has ever seen God; but if we love one another, God lives in us and His love is made complete in us.

This is how we know that we live in Him and He in us: He has given us of His Spirit. And we have seen and testify that the Father has sent His Son to be the Savior of the world. If anyone acknowledges that Jesus is the Son of God, God lives in them and they in God. And so we know and rely on the love God has for us.

God is love. Whoever lives in love lives in God, and God in them.

*When have you experienced deep, unconditional love?*

*How would you describe the way God has shown His love to people?*

*How do these verses encourage you and challenge you to love other people?*

YOU CAN GIVE
WITHOUT
*loving,*
BUT YOU CANNOT
LOVE WITHOUT
*giving.*

— Amy Carmichael

*What are some actions you can take or changes you can make to love more genuinely this week?*

*Your biggest takeaway*

# No Compromise

# PSALM 1 (CSB)

How happy is the one who does not
walk in the advice of the wicked
or stand in the pathway with sinners
or sit in the company of mockers!
Instead, his delight is in the LORD's instruction,
and he meditates on it day and night.
He is like a tree planted beside flowing streams
that bears its fruit in its season
and whose leaf does not wither.
Whatever he does prospers.

The wicked are not like this;
instead, they are like chaff that the wind blows away.
Therefore the wicked will not stand up in the judgment,
nor sinners in the assembly of the righteous.

For the LORD watches over the way of the righteous,
but the way of the wicked leads to ruin.

*What beliefs, convictions, or values are you unwilling to compromise?*

*In these verses, how does the psalmist describe a righteous person?*

*How does he describe a wicked person?*

*In this psalm, what are some of the benefits the righteous person enjoys?*

IF I WALK WITH THE *world,* I CAN'T WALK WITH *God.*

— DWIGHT L. MOODY

*How would delighting in and meditating on the Bible affect your choices in life? List areas in your life that you need God's help to stand firm and not compromise.*

---
---
---
---
---
---
---
---
---
---
---
---
---
---
---
---
---
---
---

*A note from Candace*

None of us are perfect, but Jesus stood firm in His convictions and so should we. It's not always easy to stand firm; honoring God with everything I do and say takes courage. Spending time with other Christians, reading the Bible, and praying all the time give me the daily strength I need to stay strong in my faith and not compromise what I believe.

# Joy in the Lord

# PHILIPPIANS 4:4—9 (ESV)

Rejoice in the Lord always; again I will say, rejoice. Let your reasonableness be known to everyone. The Lord is at hand; do not be anxious about anything, but in everything by prayer and supplication with thanksgiving let your requests be made known to God. And the peace of God, which surpasses all understanding, will guard your hearts and your minds in Christ Jesus.

Finally, brothers, whatever is true, whatever is honorable, whatever is just, whatever is pure, whatever is lovely, whatever is commendable, if there is any excellence, if there is anything worthy of praise, think about these things. What you have learned and received and heard and seen in me—practice these things, and the God of peace will be with you.

*When have you experienced deep joy in your life?*

*How do you think rejoicing in the Lord and praying*
*can help you to manage life's challenges differently?*

*How do your thoughts and actions influence your level of peace?*

RESTLESSNESS AND
IMPATIENCE CHANGE

*nothing*

EXCEPT OUR

*peace*

AND *joy.*

— ELISABETH ELLIOT

*Where in your life do you need to experience more of God's joy and peace?*

*If you'd like, write out a prayer, asking God to fill you with His joy and peace.*

*Your biggest takeaway*

# Peace in the Storm

# MARK 4:35—41 (NIV)

That day when evening came, He said to His disciples, "Let us go over to the other side." Leaving the crowd behind, they took Him along, just as He was, in the boat. There were also other boats with Him. A furious squall came up, and the waves broke over the boat, so that it was nearly swamped. Jesus was in the stern, sleeping on a cushion. The disciples woke Him and said to Him, "Teacher, don't You care if we drown?"

He got up, rebuked the wind and said to the waves, "Quiet! Be still!" Then the wind died down and it was completely calm.

He said to His disciples, "Why are you so afraid? Do you still have no faith?"

They were terrified and asked each other, "Who is this? Even the wind and the waves obey Him!"

*Describe an event in your life when you felt afraid, worried, or terrified.*

*What brought you peace in that situation?*

*When life gets rough, how does your trust in Jesus compare to the disciples' level of trust in Him?*

*Why do you think Jesus was able to sleep soundly through the storm?*

*Jesus*

BRINGS

*peace*

IN YOUR

*storm.*

*Instead of being fearful and worrying during the storms of life,*

*how can you be more like Jesus and maintain your peace?*

_____

_____

_____

_____

_____

_____

_____

_____

_____

_____

_____

_____

_____

_____

_____

*Your biggest takeaway*

# Forgiveness

# MATTHEW 6:9—15 (CSB)

"Therefore, you should pray like this:

> Our Father in heaven,
> Your name be honored as holy.
> Your kingdom come.
> Your will be done
> on earth as it is in heaven.
> Give us today our daily bread.
> And forgive us our debts,
> as we also have forgiven our debtors.
> And do not bring us into temptation,
> but deliver us from the evil one.

"For if you forgive others their offenses, your heavenly Father will forgive you as well. But if you don't forgive others, your Father will not forgive your offenses."

*When is it easy for you to forgive others? When is it hard? Why?*

*How does forgiving others benefit you?*

*Why do you think God wants us to forgive those who have hurt us?*

THERE IS

*hope*

IN

*forgiveness.*

— JOHN PIPER

*What can you do to forgive others more quickly? Is there someone you need to forgive right now?*

*If you'd like, write out a prayer, asking God to help you forgive that person.*

*A note from Candace*

We all experience plenty of situations where we feel offended or wronged by people. Instead of getting angry or screaming at someone, choose forgiveness and compassion. I promise you—the more you truly forgive, the easier it gets! Try it, and you'll see!

# Growing in Faith

# II PETER 1:5–11 (NLT)

In view of all this, make every effort to respond to God's promises. Supplement your faith with a generous provision of moral excellence, and moral excellence with knowledge, and knowledge with self-control, and self-control with patient endurance, and patient endurance with godliness, and godliness with brotherly affection, and brotherly affection with love for everyone.

The more you grow like this, the more productive and useful you will be in your knowledge of our Lord Jesus Christ. But those who fail to develop in this way are shortsighted or blind, forgetting that they have been cleansed from their old sins.

So, dear brothers and sisters, work hard to prove that you really are among those God has called and chosen. Do these things, and you will never fall away. Then God will give you a grand entrance into the eternal Kingdom of our Lord and Savior Jesus Christ.

*Why do you think it's important to continually grow in your faith?*

*What is the progression of spiritual maturity described in these verses?*

*Why do you think God wants us to be productive and useful?*

# SPIRITUAL MATURITY IS NOT REACHED BY THE PASSING OF *years,* BUT BY OBEDIENCE TO THE *will of God.*

— OSWALD CHAMBERS

*In which areas of your spiritual life do you need to mature and grow? What*

*are some practical things you can do to grow in these areas?*

_Your biggest takeaway_

# Persevering through Trials

# JAMES 1:2—12 (CSB)

Consider it a great joy, my brothers and sisters, whenever you experience various trials, because you know that the testing of your faith produces endurance. And let endurance have its full effect, so that you may be mature and complete, lacking nothing.

Now if any of you lacks wisdom, he should ask God—who gives to all generously and ungrudgingly—and it will be given to him. But let him ask in faith without doubting. For the doubter is like the surging sea, driven and tossed by the wind. That person should not expect to receive anything from the Lord, being double-minded and unstable in all his ways.

Let the brother of humble circumstances boast in his exaltation, but let the rich boast in his humiliation because he will pass away like a flower of the field. For the sun rises and, together with the scorching wind, dries up the grass; its flower falls off, and its beautiful appearance perishes. In the same way, the rich person will wither away while pursuing his activities.

Blessed is the one who endures trials, because when he has stood the test he will receive the crown of life that God has promised to those who love Him.

When was the last time you persevered through something difficult and didn't give up?

Based on the verses in James, how do trials benefit our faith?

According to James, when we're going through trials,
what is God willing to give us if we ask Him?

Focus ON HOW BIG YOUR God is, NOT HOW BIG YOUR TRIAL IS.

*Considering these verses, how can you change your perspective*

*and response when you experience a trial?*

_____

_____

_____

_____

_____

_____

_____

_____

_____

_____

_____

_____

_____

_____

_____

_____

*Your biggest takeaway*

# Overcoming Doubt

# JOHN 20:24–31 (NKJV)

Now Thomas, called the Twin, one of the twelve, was not with them when Jesus came. The other disciples therefore said to him, "We have seen the Lord."

So he said to them, "Unless I see in His hands the print of the nails, and put my finger into the print of the nails, and put my hand into His side, I will not believe."

And after eight days His disciples were again inside, and Thomas with them. Jesus came, the doors being shut, and stood in the midst, and said, "Peace to you!" Then He said to Thomas, "Reach your finger here, and look at My hands; and reach your hand here, and put it into My side. Do not be unbelieving, but believing."

And Thomas answered and said to Him, "My Lord and my God!"

Jesus said to him, "Thomas, because you have seen Me, you have believed. Blessed are those who have not seen and yet have believed."

And truly Jesus did many other signs in the presence of His disciples, which are not written in this book; but these are written that you may believe that Jesus is the Christ, the Son of God, and that believing you may have life in His name.

*In which areas of your life have you dealt with doubt? Why?*

*Why do you think Thomas had a hard time believing Jesus*

*had risen from the dead even though the other disciples had seen Him?*

*Why do you think Jesus said those who believe without seeing would be blessed?*

EVEN WHEN OUR *faith* IS SMALL, *the Lord* IS READY TO HELP US.

— J. C. RYLE

*What are some things you can do to hold on to your faith*

*the next time you are tempted to doubt God?*

_A note from Candace_

It's okay to wrestle with doubts—just don't stay in a dark place with those doubts. I've discovered that my doubts can lead to questions that help me find faith-strengthening answers. Look for answers about who Jesus is by reading the Bible, praying, and asking people to help you.

# The Inspired Word of God

# II TIMOTHY 3:12–17; II PETER 1:19–21 (NLT)

Everyone who wants to live a godly life in Christ Jesus will suffer persecution. But evil people and impostors will flourish. They will deceive others and will themselves be deceived.

But you must remain faithful to the things you have been taught. You know they are true, for you know you can trust those who taught you. You have been taught the holy Scriptures from childhood, and they have given you the wisdom to receive the salvation that comes by trusting in Christ Jesus. All Scripture is inspired by God and is useful to teach us what is true and to make us realize what is wrong in our lives. It corrects us when we are wrong and teaches us to do what is right. God uses it to prepare and equip His people to do every good work.

Because of that experience, we have even greater confidence in the message proclaimed by the prophets. You must pay close attention to what they wrote, for their words are like a lamp shining in a dark place—until the Day dawns, and Christ the Morning Star shines in your hearts. Above all, you must realize that no prophecy in Scripture ever came from the prophet's own understanding, or from human initiative. No, those prophets were moved by the Holy Spirit, and they spoke from God.

*What do you believe about the Bible?*

*Do you believe it's God's Word—that it comes from Him?*

*Based on these verses, how does God's Word benefit us?*

*Peter says the Bible's words are like "a lamp shining in a dark place." What does this mean to you?*

# God's Word

## IS TRUE
## WHETHER WE BELIEVE
## IT OR NOT.

— A. W. TOZER

*How can you allow the inspired Word of God to teach and guide you today?*

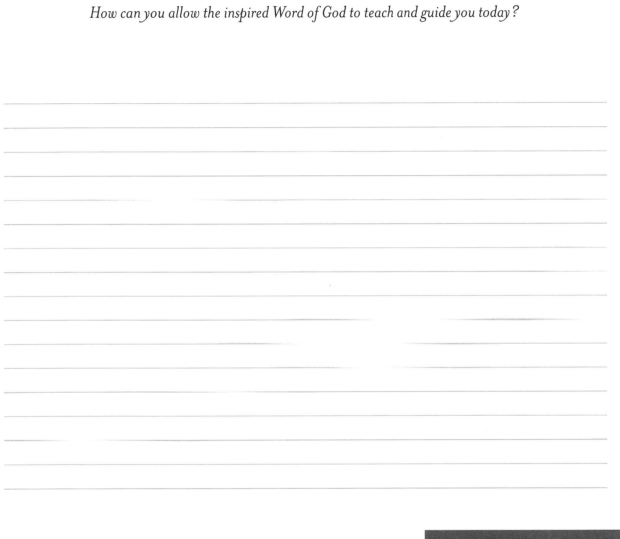

*Your biggest takeaway*

# Producing Spiritual Fruit

# GALATIANS 5:16—26 (ESV)

But I say, walk by the Spirit, and you will not gratify the desires of the flesh. For the desires of the flesh are against the Spirit, and the desires of the Spirit are against the flesh, for these are opposed to each other, to keep you from doing the things you want to do. But if you are led by the Spirit, you are not under the law. Now the works of the flesh are evident: sexual immorality, impurity, sensuality, idolatry, sorcery, enmity, strife, jealousy, fits of anger, rivalries, dissensions, divisions, envy, drunkenness, orgies, and things like these. I warn you, as I warned you before, that those who do such things will not inherit the kingdom of God. But the fruit of the Spirit is love, joy, peace, patience, kindness, goodness, faithfulness, gentleness, self-control; against such things there is no law. And those who belong to Christ Jesus have crucified the flesh with its passions and desires.

If we live by the Spirit, let us also keep in step with the Spirit. Let us not become conceited, provoking one another, envying one another.

*Christians have the presence of God—the Holy Spirit—with them.*

*How often do you think about the Holy Spirit? Why?*

*How would you describe the difference between the sinful nature's fruit and the Holy Spirit's fruit?*

*Why do you think it's so important to be guided by the Holy Spirit?*

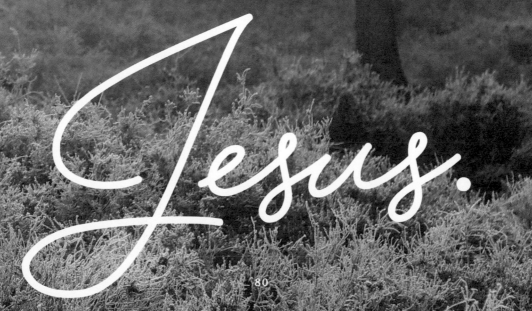

THE FRUIT OF THE

*Spirit*

IS A NATURAL RESULT

OF GROWING IN OUR

RELATIONSHIP WITH

*Jesus.*

*Which fruit of the Spirit do you need to grow in most?*

*What are some practical ways that you can intentionally grow in this area?*

Your biggest takeaway

# Generous Living

# II CORINTHIANS 9:6—15 (NLT)

Remember this—a farmer who plants only a few seeds will get a small crop. But the one who plants generously will get a generous crop. You must each decide in your heart how much to give. And don't give reluctantly or in response to pressure. "For God loves a person who gives cheerfully." And God will generously provide all you need. Then you will always have everything you need and plenty left over to share with others. As the Scriptures say,

"They share freely and give generously to the poor.
Their good deeds will be remembered forever."

For God is the One who provides seed for the farmer and then bread to eat. In the same way, He will provide and increase your resources and then produce a great harvest of generosity in you.

Yes, you will be enriched in every way so that you can always be generous. And when we take your gifts to those who need them, they will thank God. So two good things will result from this ministry of giving—the needs of the believers in Jerusalem will be met, and they will joyfully express their thanks to God.

As a result of your ministry, they will give glory to God. For your generosity to them and to all believers will prove that you are obedient to the Good News of Christ. And they will pray for you with deep affection because of the overflowing grace God has given to you. Thank God for this gift too wonderful for words!

*When was the last time someone was generous toward you?*

*How did you feel after experiencing this generosity?*

*Which of the promises in this passage stick out to you most? Why?*

*According to these verses, what are some of the results of our generosity?*

# God

LOVES A

## person

WHO GIVES

## cheerfully.

*How do these verses help you think differently about generous living?*

*In which areas of your life can you up your generosity level?*

_____
_____
_____
_____
_____
_____
_____
_____
_____
_____
_____
_____
_____
_____
_____
_____

*A note from Candace*

Generosity is contagious! And we can be generous with more than our money—we can give love, a kind word, a helping hand, or even time. But I admit—sometimes I'm guilty of being so focused on my to-do list that I forget to look for ways to surprise people with generosity. Let's be more intentional about passing along blessings to others.

# Slow to Anger

# JAMES 1:19–27 (NIV)

My dear brothers and sisters, take note of this: Everyone should be quick to listen, slow to speak and slow to become angry, because human anger does not produce the righteousness that God desires. Therefore, get rid of all moral filth and the evil that is so prevalent and humbly accept the word planted in you, which can save you.

Do not merely listen to the word, and so deceive yourselves. Do what it says. Anyone who listens to the word but does not do what it says is like someone who looks at his face in a mirror and, after looking at himself, goes away and immediately forgets what he looks like. But whoever looks intently into the perfect law that gives freedom, and continues in it—not forgetting what they have heard, but doing it—they will be blessed in what they do.

Those who consider themselves religious and yet do not keep a tight rein on their tongues deceive themselves, and their religion is worthless. Religion that God our Father accepts as pure and faultless is this: to look after orphans and widows in their distress and to keep oneself from being polluted by the world.

*When do you struggle most with anger?*

*In these verses, what does James encourage us to do? Do you struggle or excel in these areas?*

*How could an uncontrolled tongue hinder your relationship with God and your relationships with other people?*

# BE QUICK TO

## *listen,*

## SLOW TO

## *speak*

# AND SLOW TO

# BECOME ANGRY.

*What are some practical things you can do this week to help you react*

*with less anger and respond with more love to other people?*

_____

_____

_____

_____

_____

_____

_____

_____

_____

_____

_____

_____

_____

_____

*Your biggest takeaway*

# God's Power

# PSALM 62:5–12 (NLT)

Let all that I am wait quietly before God,
    for my hope is in Him.
He alone is my rock and my salvation,
    my fortress where I will not be shaken.
My victory and honor come from God alone.
    He is my refuge, a rock where no enemy can reach me.
O my people, trust in Him at all times.
    Pour out your heart to Him,
    for God is our refuge. *Interlude*

Common people are as worthless as a puff of wind,
    and the powerful are not what they appear to be.
If you weigh them on the scales,
    together they are lighter than a breath of air.

Don't make your living by extortion
    or put your hope in stealing.
And if your wealth increases,
    don't make it the center of your life.

God has spoken plainly,
    and I have heard it many times:
Power, O God, belongs to You;
    unfailing love, O Lord, is Yours.
Surely You repay all people
    according to what they have done.

*When do you feel the weakest?*

*What are some reasons David gives in this psalm for why he trusts God?*

*Which of these verses do you relate to most? Why?*

# God
## OFTEN
## SHOWCASES HIS
## power
## ON THE STAGE OF
## HUMAN WEAKNESS.

— ANDY STANLEY

*What are some things you can do this week to acknowledge God's power in your life?*

_Your biggest takeaway_

# DAY 19

# Effective Prayer

# JAMES 5:13—20 (NIV)

Is anyone among you in trouble? Let them pray. Is anyone happy? Let them sing songs of praise. Is anyone among you sick? Let them call the elders of the church to pray over them and anoint them with oil in the name of the Lord. And the prayer offered in faith will make the sick person well; the Lord will raise them up. If they have sinned, they will be forgiven. Therefore confess your sins to each other and pray for each other so that you may be healed. The prayer of a righteous person is powerful and effective.

Elijah was a human being, even as we are. He prayed earnestly that it would not rain, and it did not rain on the land for three and a half years. Again he prayed, and the heavens gave rain, and the earth produced its crops.

My brothers and sisters, if one of you should wander from the truth and someone should bring that person back, remember this: Whoever turns a sinner from the error of their way will save them from death and cover over a multitude of sins.

*How often do you pray, and what do you typically pray about? Do you only pray when you need something from God, or do you pray to strengthen your relationship with Him?*

*How do these verses help you think differently about prayer?*

*According to James, what are some of the things we should pray for?*

# WE CANNOT

## *pray*

# AND REMAIN THE

## *same.*

— RUTH GRAHAM

*Followers of Jesus can expect their prayers to be "powerful and effective."*

*What are your expectations when it comes to prayer?*

*If you'd like, write out a prayer, asking God to answer in His wisdom and with His power.*

*A note from Candace*

Since God's my best friend, I talk to Him every day. Praying keeps my thoughts and priorities focused on Him. I am constantly asking Him to guide me to do what He wants me to do and to show me how to best represent Him and His love to other people. Because I trust Him, I can pray about anything and everything.

# Wearing Your Faith

# COLOSSIANS 3:12—17 (CSB)

Therefore, as God's chosen ones, holy and dearly loved, put on compassion, kindness, humility, gentleness, and patience, bearing with one another and forgiving one another if anyone has a grievance against another. Just as the Lord has forgiven you, so you are also to forgive. Above all, put on love, which is the perfect bond of unity. And let the peace of Christ, to which you were also called in one body, rule your hearts. And be thankful. Let the word of Christ dwell richly among you, in all wisdom teaching and admonishing one another through psalms, hymns, and spiritual songs, singing to God with gratitude in your hearts. And whatever you do, in word or in deed, do everything in the name of the Lord Jesus, giving thanks to God the Father through Him.

*How much do you consider how your actions and words reflect what you say you believe?*

*According to these verses, what are some of the characteristics that followers of Jesus should "put on"?*

*How seriously do you take Paul's teaching in these verses to "do everything in the name of the Lord Jesus"? Why?*

WE ARE CITIZENS OF A
DIFFERENT KINGDOM,
AMBASSADORS
REPRESENTING
*Christ*
IN A FOREIGN LAND.

— RANDY ALCORN

*How do these verses help you think differently about "wearing" your faith wherever you go so that you accurately represent Jesus to other people?*

*Your biggest takeaway*

# Being Trustworthy

# LUKE 16:10—15 (NLT)

"If you are faithful in little things, you will be faithful in large ones. But if you are dishonest in little things, you won't be honest with greater responsibilities. And if you are untrustworthy about worldly wealth, who will trust you with the true riches of heaven? And if you are not faithful with other people's things, why should you be trusted with things of your own?

"No one can serve two masters. For you will hate one and love the other; you will be devoted to one and despise the other. You cannot serve God and be enslaved to money."

The Pharisees, who dearly loved their money, heard all this and scoffed at Him. Then He said to them, "You like to appear righteous in public, but God knows your hearts. What this world honors is detestable in the sight of God."

*Who is the most trustworthy person you know? Why do you trust this person?*

*Considering these verses, would you describe yourself as trustworthy and faithful? Why or why not?*

*How can being enslaved to money make a person unfaithful to God?*

# God

KNOWS YOUR

## heart.

*When we are trustworthy, others can count on us—and God can count on us. In what areas of your life will you work to be more trustworthy and faithful in the little things and the big things?*

_Your biggest takeaway_

# Active Faith

# JAMES 2:14—24 (NLT)

What good is it, dear brothers and sisters, if you say you have faith but don't show it by your actions? Can that kind of faith save anyone? Suppose you see a brother or sister who has no food or clothing, and you say, "Goodbye and have a good day; stay warm and eat well"—but then you don't give that person any food or clothing. What good does that do?

So you see, faith by itself isn't enough. Unless it produces good deeds, it is dead and useless.

Now someone may argue, "Some people have faith; others have good deeds." But I say, "How can you show me your faith if you don't have good deeds? I will show you my faith by my good deeds."

You say you have faith, for you believe that there is one God. Good for you! Even the demons believe this, and they tremble in terror. How foolish! Can't you see that faith without good deeds is useless?

Don't you remember that our ancestor Abraham was shown to be right with God by his actions when he offered his son Isaac on the altar? You see, his faith and his actions worked together. His actions made his faith complete. And so it happened just as the Scriptures say: "Abraham believed God, and God counted him as righteous because of his faith." He was even called the friend of God. So you see, we are shown to be right with God by what we do, not by faith alone.

*When is it hardest for you to act on your faith? Why?*

*What does the statement "faith by itself isn't enough" mean to you?*

*Why do you think it's important to back up what you believe (your faith) with your actions?*

# Faith

AND

## actions

WORK

TOGETHER.

*What are some practical things you can do this week to make sure your faith is active?*

*If you'd like, write down some "good deeds" you can do to demonstrate your faith.*

_____

_____

_____

_____

_____

_____

_____

_____

_____

_____

_____

_____

_____

_____

_____

_____

_____

*A note from Candace*

We can recite whatever Bible verses we want, but if others don't see us actively living out our faith, then we are not representing Jesus very well. I'm totally inspired when I see someone actively living out their faith—going out of their way to help another person—and it makes me want to do the same!

# Trusting in God's Character

# PSALM 23 (CSB)

The LORD is my shepherd;
I have what I need.
He lets me lie down in green pastures;
He leads me beside quiet waters.
He renews my life;
He leads me along the right paths
for His name's sake.
Even when I go through the darkest valley,
I fear no danger,
for You are with me;
Your rod and Your staff—they comfort me.

You prepare a table before me
in the presence of my enemies;
You anoint my head with oil;
my cup overflows.
Only goodness and faithful love will pursue me
all the days of my life,
and I will dwell in the house of the LORD
as long as I live.

*How has God cared for you in the past week?*

*According to these verses, how is God like a shepherd? How are you like His sheep?*

*What can you learn about God's character from these verses?*

# UNDERSTANDING

## God's

# CHARACTER MAKES

# IT EASIER TO

## trust

## Him.

*How can these verses help you to trust God more this week?*

_____

_____

_____

_____

_____

_____

_____

_____

_____

_____

_____

_____

_____

_____

_____

*Your biggest takeaway*

# The Right Kind of Fear

# PSALM 34:8–18 (NKJV)

|

Oh, taste and see that the LORD is good;

Blessed is the man who trusts in Him!

Oh, fear the LORD, you His saints!

There is no want to those who fear Him.

The young lions lack and suffer hunger;

But those who seek the LORD shall not lack any good thing.

Come, you children, listen to me;

I will teach you the fear of the LORD.

Who is the man who desires life,

And loves many days, that he may see good?

Keep your tongue from evil,

And your lips from speaking deceit.

Depart from evil and do good;

Seek peace and pursue it.

The eyes of the LORD are on the righteous,

And His ears are open to their cry.

The face of the LORD is against those who do evil,

To cut off the remembrance of them from the earth.

The righteous cry out, and the LORD hears,

And delivers them out of all their troubles.

The LORD is near to those who have a broken heart,

And saves such as have a contrite spirit.

*Fearing the Lord is another way to say "respecting the Lord."*

*Do you feel like you fear the Lord? Why or why not?*

*What actions do people take when they fear the Lord?*

*According to these verses, what are some results of fearing the Lord?*

THE FEAR OF

*the Lord*

IS THE

BEGINNING OF

*wisdom.*

— PROVERBS 9:10

*How can you actively demonstrate that you fear the Lord this week?*

_____

_____

_____

_____

_____

_____

_____

_____

_____

_____

_____

_____

_____

_____

_____

_____

*A note from Candace*

Fearing God isn't about being afraid of God—it's about acknowledging His greatness and our smallness. It's about honoring Him above ourselves. I've found that when I fear God, I make better decisions, remain humble, and treat people better.

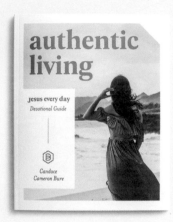